Maa माँ
Mother

R.N. Kogata • Lalita Kogata

D.K. Printworld (P) Ltd.
New Delhi

Cataloging in Publication Data — DK
[Courtesy: D.K. Agencies (P) Ltd. <docinfo@dkagencies.com>]

Kogata, R. N. (Ram Narayan), 1964–
Maa = Mother / R.N. Kogata, Lalita Kogata.
p. cm.
English and Hindi.
ISBN 13: 9788124604571
ISBN 10: 8124604576

1. Mothers — Prayers and devotions. 2. Mothers and sons. 3. Mothers in art. 4. Parvati (Hindu deity) — Art. 5. Gaṇeśa (Hindu deity) — Art. 6. Art, Hindu. I. Kogata, Lalita, 1965–, joint author. II. Title. III. Title: Mother.

DDC 306.874 3 22

First Published in India, 2009
ISBN 13: 978-81-246-0457-1
ISBN 10: 81-246-0457-6

A Creation of:
Mr. R.N. Kogata
Mrs. Lalita Kogata
608, Hiran Magari, Sector-11, Udaipur - India
Phone : +91-94141-58870
devkush@rediffmail.com

Published and printed by:
D.K. Printworld (P) Ltd.
'Sri Kunj' F-52, Bali Nagar
Ramesh Nagar Metro Stn., New Delhi - 110015
Phs.: 011-2545 3975, 2546 6019
Fax: 011-2546 5926
Email: dkprintworld@vsnl.net
Web: www.dkprintworld.com

Maa माँ Mother

उपाध्यायन्दशाचार्य आचार्याणां शतं पिता।
सहस्रं तु पितृन्माता गौरवेणातिरिच्यते।।
— मनुस्मृति, 2.145

गौरव की दृष्टि से दस उपाध्यायों की अपेक्षा आचार्य, सौ आचार्यों की अपेक्षा पिता और सहस्रों पिताओं से माता का गौरव अधिक होता है।

Preceptor is ten times greater than teacher; father is a hundred times greater than preceptor; and mother is a thousand times greater than father.

॥ ॐ गं गणपतये नमः ॥

Preface

Matridevobhav ! Look upon your mother as God. God cannot be everywhere, so he created Mother. A mother is the closest relative of any person and therefore it is said - "Tule Na Tahi Sakal Sambandhi" which means no relative can be compared with mother in any respect. A mother takes a lot of pain to give birth, bring up a child, she is the first teacher for the child, loves her child in all circumstances, saves her child from all the evils and Mother is the first word spoken by anyone in the life.

Suktimala, 593 describes five women as Mother — own mother without whom any-one's existence is impossible, your wife's mother who gives her daughter for life to you, the wife of King as he is said to be representative of God and protects people, elder brother's wife as she acts as Mother in the absence of your own Mother and teacher's wife as teacher is like God as described in *Hari-Hara Subhashita,* 3.3.

Maa — Mother! this word not only gives great feelings and reflection of sweetness of love, affection, respect, blessings, faith, belief, mercy, kindness, warmth and so on but also gives heroism and fame and is the symbol of sacrifice and penance.

For Mother, her child always remains a child at all ages may it be Human or God. Mother is the name for God in the lips and hearts of little children. Mother is compared with Tridev - Brahma, Vishnu and Mahesh. The success of any person has compulsory ingredients of moral, intellectual and physical education from the Mother. What Mother does for us cannot be done by anyone else and no one can replace Mother in any way.

Inspired by these heart-touching facts, we did a small attempt in 2004 with the blessings of His Highness Shreeji Arvind Singh Mewar in the form of a book on "Maa - the mother" to express our thoughts about Mother and we would always be grateful to him. We are grateful to Dr M.L. Swarankar, Chairman, India Education Trust, Jaipur for his whole-hearted support. We are also grateful to all our wellwishers and readers, who have made the first and second edition a great success and have given us an opportunity to come out with this third edition of the book so quickly.

Our real success are those heart touching letters, which we have received from some of our readers expressing their view that this book has totally changed their thinking and respect towards the mother, which they could not fully realize before reading this book. We feel that if we can change even few people, the God has fulfilled our wishes and object.

We prostrate before our parents for their beloved blessings for reaching this stage. We are also thankful to learned poet Shri Om Vyas "OM" from Ujjain for his poem on Mother. He is an internationally known and renowned Poet writing since 1970, and besides whole of India, he has presented his jewels of poems in USA, Dubai, Sharjah and Nepal also.

As usual, with the expectation of blessing from all of you.

R.N. Kogata
Lalita Kogata

Importance of Mother

Taittiriya Upanishad says *Maatridevo bhava* — consider your mother as a god. In Tamil country, Avvaiyaar, a poetess, said "Mother and father are your visible gods." *Devi Mahaatmyam* has a shloka *"yaa devi sarva bhuteshu maatri roopena samsthithaa . . ."* Devi Durga resides in all beings in the form of mother. *Manusmriti* says, "*aachaarya* (preceptor) is ten times greater than a teacher who imparts knowledge for a fee, Father is a hundred times greater than an *aachaarya*, and Mother is a thousand times greater than a father."

From all these quotes from scriptures we know how exalted a position mother holds in our society.

We identify mother with all the good qualities like caring for us, giving nourishment, patiently bearing all troubles and sustaining us at all times. We thus worship neem tree and tulsi plant as mother, cow as mother, earth as mother and river as mother. In other words, we see mother in all things in life. Why, when we get some money from someone we even say "Maa Lakshmi has come."

Aadi Shankaracharya has said in one shloka, "there can be bad children, but never a bad mother." Mother, in the true sense of the word, can only be good.

Mother always thinks good for her children. Her aim in life is to see that her children grow up and become good, intelligent and successful persons.

The first word a baby utters, whether in India or anywhere abroad, is "maa." Then comes amma, mummy, mother, mom, etc. While walking we hit a stone, it pains and we immediately say "maa." We say "Vande Mataram," i.e. we offer our pranaams to our motherland, as we see our country as a mother.

It is good to see that we think of mother at all times. But, do we really care for our mother in her old age? If we look at the growth of old-age homes even in villages, we have to conclude that some parents in their old age are not cared for by their children at all. This is a very sad state of affairs.

According to a story in the *Mahabharata*, a boy who neglected his parents, learnt some *mantra*s and thought that he had attained great powers. When he was sitting under a tree a bird's dropping fell on him. He looked up with anger, and the bird was burnt to ashes. The boy thought that he had attained *mantrashakti*, that there was no need for him to do any service, and that his *mantrashakti* would make others serve him. When he was feeling hungry, he went to a house and asked for some food. The lady of the house was busy in looking after her husband and his old parents and so did not answer the boy. The boy showed anger, but the lady said "I am not a bird to be burnt by you." The boy was surprised, forgot his hunger, and asked the lady how she knew about the bird. She simply told him "There is a butcher at the end of the village, go and ask him." Baffled, the boy went to the butcher. The butcher had no time to talk to the boy. The boy waited patiently. Then the butcher asked the boy "Has a lady sent you here?" The boy was more baffled and asked the butcher how he knew about the lady. After finishing his business, the butcher went to his house, bathed his old parents, gave them meals and attended to their comforts. After serving them, the butcher came and told the boy, "That lady was doing service to her husband and parents-in-law. Because of that virtue she could see the past, present and future, and so she knew about the bird. As far as I am concerned, my gods are in my house only, i.e. my mother and father. I serve them to their satisfaction, and because of this virtue I know about the lady and the bird. What have you done? Yours *mantra* is just worth a paisa. There are *mantra*s for snake-bite, scorpion-bite etc., and your *mantra*s are also like that. For getting God's blessings, you need not know any *mantra*s, it is enough if you serve your mother and father."

Our Puranas and Shastras contain many such examples. They emphasize the point that doing one's duty is of the highest importance and earns all virtues — that is, duties of the wife to the husband, the son to his parents, and so on.

bhoopradakshina shadgena
kaasiyaatraayute nasa ।
sethu snaana sathairyascha
tatphalam maatruvandane ।।

The virtue you get by going round the earth six times,
Ten thousand times bathing in the holy Ganges,
Many many times doing *snaana* at Rameshwaram,
All these virtues you get if you sincerely Prostrate before your mother once.

माँ! माँ संवेदना है, भावना है, अहसास है।
माँ! माँ जीवन के फूलों में खुशबू का वास है।।

Maa ! Mother is an emotion, a thought, a kind feeling.
Maa ! Mother is the fragrance of the flower of life.

माँ! माँ रोते हुए बच्चे का खुशनुमा पन्ना है।
माँ! माँ मरूस्थल में नदी, एक मीठा सा झरना है।।

Maa ! Mother is the pleasant page of a crying child.
Maa ! Mother is a river in the desert & also a sweet water fall.

माँ! माँ लोरी है, गीत है, प्यारी सी थाप है।
माँ! माँ पूजा की थाली, मंत्रों का जाप है।।

Maa माँ Mother

Maa ! Mother is a lullaby, sweet song and a lovely soft pat on the back.
Maa ! Mother is a shield of worship and silent reading of chants.

माँ! माँ आँखों का सिसकता हुआ किनारा है।
माँ! माँ गालों पर पप्पी है, ममता की धारा है।।

Maa ! Mother is an overflowing edge of tears.
Maa ! Mother is a sweet kiss on the cheeks
and an unending stream of love & affection.

माँ! माँ सुलगते दिलों में कोयल की बोली है।
माँ! माँ मेहंदी है, कुमकुम है, सिंदुर है, रोली है।।

Maa माँ Mother

Maa ! Mother is a sweet voice of cuckoo in the burning heart.
Maa ! Mother is henna, kumkum, sindoor and roli.

माँ! माँ कलम है, दवात है, स्याही है।
माँ! माँ परमात्मा की स्वयं एक गवाही है।।

Maa ! Mother is a writing reed, is an inkpot and also ink.
Maa ! Mother itself is a witness of the almighty.

माँ! माँ त्याग है, तपस्या है, सेवा है।
माँ! माँ फूंक से ठंडा किया हुआ कलेवा है।।

Maa माँ Mother

Maa ! Mother is sacrifice, penance and service.
Maa ! Mother is a sweet, cool, tasty & hygienic dish of food.

माँ! माँ अनुष्ठान है, प्रार्थना है, जीवन का हवन है।
माँ! माँ हमारे जीवन के मोहल्ले में आत्मा का भवन है।।

Maa माँ Mother

Maa ! Mother is an objective religious ceremony,
a prayer and fire offerings of the life.
Maa ! Mother is the soul of the house in the colony of life.

माँ! माँ चूड़ी वाले हाथों के मजबूत कंधों का नाम है।
माँ! माँ काशी है, काबा है और चारों धाम है।।

Maa ! Mother is the name of strong shoulders
of the arms wearing bangles.
Maa ! Mother is Kashi, Kaba and also all four holy places.

माँ! माँ चिंता है, प्यार है, हिचकी है।
माँ! माँ बच्चे की हर चोट पर सिसकी है।।

Maa ! Mother is the name of care, love and symbol of remembrance.
Maa ! Mother sobs on every wound of the child.

माँ! माँ चूल्हा, धुँआ, रोटी और हाथों का छाला है।
माँ! माँ ज़िंदगी की कड़वाहट में अमृत का प्याला है।।

Maa मॉं Mother

Maa ! Mother is a hearth, smoke, bread and a blister on the palm.
Maa ! Mother is the nectar bowl in the bitterness of the life.

माँ! माँ पृथ्वी है, जगत है, धुरी है।
माँ! माँ बिना इस सृष्टि की कल्पना अधूरी है।।

Maa माँ Mother

Maa ! Mother is the earth, the universe and the center of gravity.
Maa ! Mother - the imagination of this universe
is impossible without Mother.

माँ! माँ की ये कथा अनादि है, यह अध्याय नहीं है।
माँ! माँ का जीवन में कोई पर्याय नहीं है।।

Maa ! Mother's altogether different story comes
from ancient times and is not mere a chapter.
Maa ! Mother - there is no synonym of mother in any one's life.

माँ! माँ का महत्व कम हो नहीं सकता।
माँ! माँ जैसा दुनिया में कुछ हो नहीं सकता।।

Maa ! Mother - the importance of Mother is unending and can never go down. Maa ! Mother - no one in the world can become or replace Mother in any way.

ईश्वर, अल्ला, राम लिखा। ईसा, रब, सतनाम लिखा।।
हर बच्चे ने हर पन्ने पर। माँ को ही प्रणाम लिखा।।
शर्त लगी सारी दुनियाँ को। एक शब्द में लिखने की।।
सबने सब कुछ ही लिख डाला। मैंने माँ का नाम लिखा।।

M - Million things she gave me
O - Outstanding & Incomparable in all respect
T - Tears she shed to save me
H - Heart of purest gold
E - Eyes with love light shining
R - Right and right she'll always be

Put them all together and it will spell MOTHER.
A WORD that means the WORLD to us.

God has given every Mother -
Fortitude, Courage, Tolerance, Flexibility,
Patience, Firmness, Sacrifice, Blessings, love,
Affection, Faith, Belief, Kindness, Mercy and
nearly every other brave aspect of the human soul.

Maa माँ Mother

A Mother is the truest friend we have—
When trials, heavy and sudden, fall upon us,
When friends who rejoice with us in our sunshine desert us,
When troubles thicken around us,
Under all circumstances, she will cling to us and endeavor
by her kind precepts and counsels to dissipate the
clouds of darkness and cause peace to return to our hearts.